SIT QUIETLY.

LISTEN LOUDLY.

Kellie Fellinge

Author's Note

When we have questions, the answers don't always come in linear messages. The awareness you need will arrive and you will connect ideas, thoughts and your wisdom.

Trust yourself.

Use the passages in this volume as you need them. Flip around as I do when I am compelled to capture an idea on the page. Perhaps a single word will resonate with you today, or a passage will lead you to deeper reflection. Read cover to cover or follow the sequence of the index. What you need at any given time will find you.

1

SIT.

2

LISTEN.

What you listen for, the messages you are waiting to find, don't come in any logical order but they come in the order you need. A lesson may marinate in your memory for years before you need it to partner with new wisdom earned through hard work and paying attention. What doesn't make sense today, may be perfectly clear in a year, or ten. Allow yourself the grace to receive, to listen, and to absorb as it comes. Pay attention and keep the lessons tucked safely away in your tool bag for when it is time to use them.

4

ABSORB.

Do you stare at the blank page too? The only cure is to begin. Make a mark. The question of the blank page was before me this morning, so I began with an observation. It is a fear of the void. A fear of what we may find in the cavern of our thoughts. Our own minds are possibly also a blank page. The amount of thought and ideas is endless. You could never fit it all on the page and so it remains a question of where to start. The possibilities of what we find when we begin the discovery is scary, but it is a journey worth taking.

BE.

Once you discover your first moment of listening, it is like the first delectable taste of a well-made treat, and you will want more. Once your patience and grace breaks through and you are able to listen, you will know the steps to get there again. Be gentle with your thoughts. Like a new pair of boots, you will get blisters in your practice of listening. Eventually you will walk for miles and for days in your boots. Eventually you will break free of the noise and find yourself able to listen.

8

TRUST.

The cat has curled her head under on my lap in complete, vulnerable surrender to her slumber. In complete relaxation in her trust. The cat has indicated she longs to nap, and I can be her guardian of protection from any predators. Who is my guardian of protection? When do I slumber as easily as the cat? With the unrest of the world, distraction and division, when do I slumber unencumbered?

10

PUZZLE.

The rain in the early morning field captured by the grasses is devoured by the roots below as plants drink the sparkling drops. In the muted colors of dawn, the world looks groggy. The colors are not vibrant. It is all half asleep, before the sun rises over the horizon. It is in this space where I process. I allow the thoughts, worries and wisdom to weave through my mind, finding my way.

12

COMFORT.

Rhythm is important to the human soul - the vibration, the soothing that comes from some repetitive movement. Perhaps it is the mother's heartbeat that sets in motion this need. We find solace in predictable, repeatable action or sounds like a rocking chair or knitting. Run, walk, swim, tap, hum, metronomes, even perhaps the bumps on a familiar highway are all soothing repetitive motion. Lovely and relaxing. Whatever your action of choice, however fast or slow, find your rhythm often.

14

STOP.

Sound sleep regulates your mood and your gut. Sleep keeps your brain free of clutter and your thoughts organized. When our thoughts are racing and mind is full, when our body is aching and sore – sleep is more elusive. Moderation in all things, day in and day out is appropriate to the needs of our sleep. That leaves little room for novelty, adventure or discovery. So perhaps the occasional night of lost sleep over something new and exciting is ok, but let's cheer on our evenings for more refreshing consistency and better sleep.

SHARPEN.

In the fever dreams of illness what really comes to light is what is important. The lists, to dos, crisis -all fade when the body and mind are consumed with heat and recovery. It is as if the soul is fueling the flames of illness with the scrap and nonsense to light what is truly important. As if we need to do a strategic burn of all the non-essentials to prevent a larger burnout of our bodies. For when we pull through the intensity, it takes a moment to mend, to begin a regrowth of only the strongest parts of what we are meant to do.

18

WARM.

When the brain spirals of thought send you into a tailspin, and you get out of control, it is hard to stop. Like the spinning teacups of a carnival ride, spinning around on the saucer which is also spinning around in a circle. This loss of control means you get flung about and spit out into the fray. The best way to avoid that is don't forget to breathe. A breath, a pause, a moment of reflection keeps you holding on.

ADORE.

Rituals offer an opportunity to pause, reflect, transfer oneself to the next phase. Intended to mark a point in time, rituals need not be elaborate. A ritual may be a quiet welcoming of your day, or a transition into your week. It may be a regular cleansing of your home/body/workspace. There may be ritual in your art practice or your run. Encourage a ritual, a small practice of appreciation for your day.

22

SCENT.

There is creaking in the floor and my shoulders bristle with the knowledge the day will begin soon. This moment will give way to meals and to meetings and things to do and places to go. This is magic right here, the early hours. Whether slumbering in your covers or brewing your coffee in the quiet dark, these hours are for each of us. It is silent. We can think without input. We can hear ourselves and listen to what we know.

CALM.

I currently live in the reality the coffee is either decaf or it is half caf, and I am not sure it matters which is true. I could create any truth from the facts I have and create the reality I choose. Isn't that the case with all our goings on. We only ever have a portion of any given set of facts from which to draw our conclusions, and so we do our best. But in the end here we are anyway. Our reality is what is now. Regardless of what came before, I have this pen and journal and a cat in my lap. And the coffee, which is hot, decaf or not.

LISTEN.

What makes each of us in our experience focus on the things we do. What small transgression happened in our lives that creates these specific biases one way or another. What must we do all our lives to accommodate a dislike of a style, taste, mannerism. Perhaps it is even residual from a previous experience tucked deep within our very structure to travel with us through all our days, and all our future selves – stuck with these tics that define our existence.

WITHIN.

One of my favorite breathing exercises is box breath. Take it super slow. Picture a box in the air:

Start on the corner and breathe the length of the box deep and full 1,2,3,4. Sit with the breath a moment. Then breathe the box out as you turn the corner 1,2,3,4. As your lungs empty, sit with that a moment. Turn the next corner and repeat, 1,2,3,4 - following the sides of the box slowly, with intention.

GRIEVE.

Loose yourself in the total absorption of your hands being busy with working, creating, building. Allow yourself attention on the magic of tending to something three dimensional that you can hold in your physical space. Put your attention fully on this work with your hands. They are underused; they remember more than the tiny tapping and scrolling that makes up the majority of their work.

TASTE.

When you learn to sit quietly, you begin afraid. Afraid of what you might hear. Afraid of the thoughts that might scare you, that you tucked away in your closet long ago. But that is only what you hear. That is the noise, and the noise is deafening. Rather than let the noise chase you to the dark corners, rather than let the noise scare you in the dark hours, turn off the noise. What you want to do is listen. Listen loudly. For when you listen there is only love.

PUZZLE.

When we seek adventure, often we search outside, looking to somewhere far away. We seek the answer that surely must be there if we travel far and wide. If we leave our dailies behind and only look around us perhaps we will find. Too bad it happens that we look and do not see. Too bad it happens we hear and do not listen. We eat and do not taste. We move too fast to slow down and enjoy the world that lies within us: connecting our thoughts and healing.

36

INK.

The power of the cat in your lap is greater than any willpower you may have to go, go and do the things to be done. The cat is a reminder that we do not need to rush in this moment. We do not need to hurry past this small opportunity to relax. What we have before us is this moment to reflect, for the cat does not stay out of obligation. The cat will leave at the moment she is no longer in repose. So, the challenge is to match the energy of the cat and keep her with you as long as you can, to benefit from a small moment of the slow life.

NATURE.

It is ok to sometimes sit and stare at the page. Words will come. You must capture them when they do, even if they are not the words you expected. Allowing the words to reveal themselves gives your mind space to loosen all you know – to try the pieces on and see what fits. Just sit with your pen at the ready and start placing letters on the page. It is a stretch, a warmup for your brain. And when you have captured what burbles to the surface you will start to get to the good stuff.

START.

I frequently muse that Chaos and Mischief are always with me. Isn't that true for all of us. At any moment our day may erupt in a random and unexpected way, it may derail our entire idea of what today looks like. And some days we get through while Chaos sleeps quietly waiting to be launched. Mischief can be a bit more persistent. In small ways getting into trouble, demanding a little attention to be paid, often getting louder when you don't get the joke, making sure you hear her coming with a present for you.

EMBRACE.

We all have wisdom inherently within the combined experience of the lives we have lived to look beyond this physical space and time. I know what I have lived. I know I have abandoned thoughts and experiences that have not been required or that have been built upon for finer mastery. But rather than my knowledge limited to these lived experiences, I know so much more when I listen deeply. When I listen loudly. I know all that is important already and yet it is my purpose to discover it yet again.

SEE.

45

The room has become cold, the heat has not yet come on, the cat has gone, and the coffee is empty. The muse is still with me, the words flowing freely waiting for me to capture them with my pen. There are so many things I could capture but words often aren't enough to do so, and in that case I must just welcome and absorb it all.

COLOR.

You never can tell when an interaction can change your life. A stranger on a plane. A guy waiting in line at Walmart. It is through interacting with the people who inhabit this earth with us that we find our guides. That one moment when we listen instead of judge. The energy sent to share a bit of wisdom that you have not yet found on your path. A spark that can connect the areas of your life that felt like silos. You never can tell when the person you wouldn't give a second thought about has the answer.

RELAX.

I do not pretend to be a scholar, but I know. I do not have the dates and publications at the tip of my tongue, but I know. I know deep within my cells. I know because it is the wisdom of many lives. It is the knowledge we so haphazardly bury in our daily lives beneath layers of guilt and judgement, under the dust of second guessing and the grime of competition. The cleaning and clearing and uncovering is hard.

FILL.

The words don't matter, the practice does. For as you start and try, it will feel frustrating. It will feel pointless. It will feel unsurmountable.

Try Again.

Each time you will learn one small thing. Your mind will adapt. It may slow down but it must speed with excitement first, like a dog with zoomies. Then you can quiet your mind to a resting state. Allow yourself to try without pressure. Try only with curiosity and wonder.

PLANT.

Our histories are like paper towns. Places you see on a map of your mind but don't exist in your life. Your fondness for a flavor, your love of a color exists in your energy's memory, leaving its mark on your journey, creating a route that only you can follow. Only you know what's true for your guidebook. Only you have walked that way and can mark the places you have been.

SLOW DOWN.

Once in a while you come across something magical that changes your world view. That aha moment, perhaps even occasionally called enlightenment. This moment where your perception changes happens when you are aware. When you are an active participant. You must be open to an experience, willing to take it in, not wearing your blinders. When you experience the moment with your whole self, you can live in the magic forever.

LISTEN.

Do you lose the occasional thought to the wind? It's there as you place your pen on the page and disappears as soon as the first letter is formed. Our conundrum begins with pausing to wonder what that letter is meant for. The brain scrambles but the trick is simple. As quickly as possible find a new thought beginning with that letter, by the time you finish the sentence you will have another thought that ties it together. For as surely as you lost your thought, the wind carries others to you.

EXPLORE.

We followed three miles of rope along I-5. It started with a clump, we soon realized it was unspooling along the highway like a long train of thought that you start in a conversation – messy at first and then it flows smoothly and follows a predictable line – right down the center, but suddenly the thought ends, the spool is empty, the rope is finite. And then we caught up to the truck with the empty spool and the story begins again.

SILENCE.

I am wondering where the cows in the valley go when I don't see them. All summer they are a friendly greeting to a different side of life, and then suddenly in Fall they are gone. They are big cows, so it's hard to think they are hiding. There are a lot of cows, so I doubt they go in for the night to get out of the weather. There aren't many calves, so I don't think they are tending the nursery. They just disappear in the Autumn and return the next spring like tulips.

LAUGH.

So then one day you sit down and put a word on a page, because that word belongs there. Suddenly another word comes to mind, and you find a page for it. Repeat that inspiration and excitement over and over again until there are no more pages. A challenge to only repeat the most important word, and to find the words that belong on each page. And it just happens that way sometimes when you listen.

ALLOW.

There aren't many places to go on any given morning at 3am. What you can be certain of is that everyone on the road needs to get somewhere. An early shift, an airport run, a response to a middle of the night call. They aren't going to the grocery store, or to return a pair of jeans. The 3am drivers are dedicated to their cause, moving along with traffic, keeping to their task without distraction. The calm in the world at 3am makes me want to set my alarm for 2:55.

GROW.

I have never been firmly rooted in my being. I've hidden in the shadows and been on the edge of the snapshot. I care not to be the star of the show. I caught a glimpse in the mirror and saw myself. I saw the me hidden behind curtains. I saw my Oz and knew that it was not me. It was time to change.

REMEMBER.

A morning in the chilly dark, a second cup of coffee fueling the thoughts and lighting the muse is a morning well spent. Another dollop of cream is best for the effort, its rich creaminess holding the bitter darkness of the coffee in its hand making every sip feel like the comfort of a warm sweater on a cool fall afternoon. Thoughts captured in the dark of an early morning flow with an ease that is hard to capture when the events of the day confuse them.

DISCOVER.

As you peel the papery tough protective layer of the onion, the beauty of the fragrance can make you cry. How does such a thin layer, so easily scarred and ripped also remain so strong and secure. The outer layers can be bitter, and the sweetest part is found in the center. If you look carefully that is where the new growth is. Buried deep within, the potential for more.

STILLNESS.

Your day will not be spent in silence. You need not listen loudly all the time. Practice and it will come easier. Don't limit yourself to one space. You may find stillness in unexpected places, in noisy places. You may find stillness in happy places and beautiful places. You may want to listen in the ugly places. Practice and you will find the silence to bear when you need it in the sad places and especially in the angry places. There are no dues. There is no instructor. You will find what you need when you listen.

LOVE.

Sit quietly. Listen loudly. In this early morning time, in the silence of the dark – it is so much easier to hear. So much easier to know. The thoughts arrive solid and true. Truths can be found of all the universal rules, more solid than facts. In the energy there are no alternate facts. There is truth and there is love. And there is enough for <u>all of us</u>. But we don't hear because there is noise. Others who don't hear make more noise because their silence is deafening to them. They must learn to sit quietly in their own time.

LISTEN.

There is beauty in mathematical structures – the symmetry, the straightforward answers that are provided to explain our world. Take the symmetry of the Golden Rule/Phi/The Golden Ratio/ The Fibonacci Spiral. This magical ratio of 1.6180339887. The most amazing thing is you don't need to know the rule to experience it. All you need is to look, really look in nature and it is there. Leaves and petals, plants and the bodies of creatures. It's all there waiting for your discovery and wonder.

MOVE.

A tree fell in the forest, and I cannot see its top amongst the canopy. I do not know exactly where it stood, swaying in the gentle wind. I do not know how many rings I could count across its middle.

A tree fell in the forest, I stumbled upon it as it lay in my path, its weight reshaping the land, its trunk giving a home to countless critters, its needles and branches feeding the earth surrounding it.

A tree fell in the forest. A man cut him down. I asked the man to. It was sick. It was time to let go.

DISCOVER.

Let there be a last word. Once the word has been spoken, it has done its job. Maybe it came out crooked, or perhaps you did not finish. Leave it there. Do not let the sound of your words fill your head with noise. Do not allow the record player to stick and repeat. That is giving away your valuable space at bargain basement prices. Let the words remain, settle into the dust. Let the words be. Leave the space for new thoughts. Allow new connections. Listen.

PAINT.

In the 80's all we had was long conversation. Checking of media and status was not in our palms constantly, it was maybe on the news stand and referred to people far away. These personalities did not infiltrate our minds. They did not lull us to sleep or keep us awake with their constant streams of consciousness becoming our own thoughts. Think of the impact this has. Where is the room for our own pondering and discovery. Where is the space for our wandering thought taking us somewhere new.

FEEL.

What makes each of us who we are is so beautiful. What makes me who I am today and who I am tomorrow is so magical. Imagine how everything I do, try, see, hear, taste, experience – changes me. I can never walk the same path. My routines – as lovely as I think they are – are never really the same because I have changed in each moment. Think of the opportunity that each day you are new. Each day you grow and refine. Each day you can slough off the pieces you don't like. It is inevitable and exciting to think of the impact to meet yourself again.

PLAY.

I shake when it rings true. I chill when the message is received and I get it right. The wisdom of ages swirling in my head. The characters of a foreign language dancing; yet it is in darkness that it can be read easiest. The knowing is powerful and gives me such strength but not strength over you. Strength in experience. Strength to carry with me on this journey that surely has just begun. All the experiences, all the knowing I have stored through the long winter. It is spring.

88

SUPPORT.

Be there for yourself as you are there for others. Be kind to yourself and love each little thing. Our days will pass whether we hate or love. Our days will fly whether we distract ourselves or whether we pay 100% attention. We will end up in the middle, we won't be perfect and we don't expect that of others. I hold myself in reverence. It was not always that way. Many years I didn't give myself a second thought. There is time to make up.

Third eye open to the wonders of the world. We cannot see nor can we hear. We cannot taste, nor touch, nor smell. Third eye open to what we know to be true and possible. Third eye lives within us and is in all ways watching. Always telling us what we need to know. Why do we so often ignore, not pay attention to the wisdom of the third eye. It is proof of life beyond this realm, where humans only experience a speck of the possibilities available to us. The weight of all that happens around us, the weight second guesses are particularly heavy. But we don't need to dwell on those with the third eye open. We already know and just need to pay attention to what the third eye is telling us.

I started down a path to enjoy a story – excited about subtle references to ideas that I have been swirling in my head recently. Open to finding connections to areas of my studies and contemplation. Validation of my beliefs. The story soon took me on a path of discovery, it unlocked some of the painful places I thought I was done with. I wasn't done. I had locked this place up tight. I allowed myself to travel along with the story, falling in love with the characters. Allowing it to open my dark spaces. It was the right story when I needed it.

LOOK.

The sun broke through those deep dark clouds, offering me warmth at the end of a long, cold, rainy day. The sun showed me the light exists even when the darkness is deep. Warmth can be found in the coldest of places.

In my saddest sorrows there is a golden light to show me the way when I can open my eyes again. In the coldest hours it will warm me when I have shivered.

The clouds may come, and the clouds will go. Meanwhile the sun still shines.

TRY.

I find myself staring at the caramel color of my coffee completely enraptured by the very perfect color of its rich golden hue. It has distracted me most of the morning as I capture the mundane goings on of my daily life in my early morning journal. It surprised me how perfect a color it is when Stanley poured it into my empty white cup. What amazed me even more is how in the corner of my eye this color appeared on objects all around. This perfect, ideal hue. And I never saw it.

NURTURE.

Today is the day! Did you hear? It is the only day. So, what are you going to do with it? We don't know. The day begins as a blank slate and the world splatters its color all over the place. What will you do with the paintballs of life coming your way? Some will hit you and wake you up. Some will hurt. Some will miss you but hit your day and create a rainbow. Some will create a chaos of color to clean up. The shadows of black and gray paint may cover your vision. Wipe it off and see what else can be done to clean up this mess of wonder and color. Life.

MATTER.

Welcome back foggy mornings and cobwebs. Welcome back chilly walks and soggy leaves. I did not see the changes for years. I did not experience the cold on my face or in my bones. Once I realized I missed it – so many opportunities to see the change of the season – to marvel at the resilience of the growth in spring and the absolute necessity of dormancy in winter – once I realized, I take every opportunity to stop and marvel.

LISTEN.

Why are we so prone to distraction. What makes us so easily diverted from our task to something shiny in the corner. There is such grace and calm with the predictable nature of routine. Our stress levels stay down. Our heart rate stays slow. Our smiles are genuine. The newest, brightest attracts us as novelty but is so much easier discarded, where the tried and true remains. Tend to what slows you down. Tend to what allows some focus, not to the latest and greatest that you will soon abandon.

102

MAGIC.

The forest is breath. It breathes out so that you may breathe in. The forest is life. Always growing, taking its time, following the cycles. Never in a hurry and always on time. The moss and the cedar each with its job, allowing each other to exist, creating what others need, taking only what is necessary. A path through the forest is a wonderland protecting you from both rain and sun. Changing every day as the berries grow, as the leaves fall. The forest is death. Giving itself back to the earth to nurture life.

GENTLE.

A thickening spiral of thought takes a worry and each time you go full circle thinking about it, your spiral gets thicker and denser like a mortar in stone. It becomes harder to free yourself from the continuous cycles. The spiral grows bigger, heavier – unmanageable, unrecognizable. The thickening spiral soon weighs more than you can carry – its burden unbearable.

INVITE.

We are born an empty vessel formed from the cells of our past into the experience of this world. This world is full of learnings and offers up many things to fill our mind and crowd our emotions. The wisdom of the ages in this world are dandelion puffs waiting to waft our direction and seed their knowledge into our minds. Too often we blow them away, not paying attention, a nuisance distracting us from our shiny things and pursuits. These puffs of wisdom are what we are looking for.

READ.

In any moment of joy there may also exist fear. In those moments of fear, you may find anger or a grief. Sometimes grief brings with it a drop of relief, for no moment is yes or no. No moment is right or wrong. Your relief may also be flooded with joy. You may experience all the emotion at once so fast that it overwhelms. You may see that guilt accompanies many experiences like a nagging shadow, like a gray cloud above your head. Throw up your umbrella, turn on the light. Not today.

CONSIDER.

What is our time missing out on in service to the foe of distraction. Constant distraction keeps us from our own journey of experience and discovery. If we watch instead of do, if we take input of what others tell us, we are not listening to our own wisdom. The wisdom, the answers, the guidance is there waiting for us when we take out the ear buds and have our own interactions with the world and within ourselves.

INHALE.

As the thoughts become clearer, as the practice becomes true, the words flow through my pen from a space that seems to bypass my being. There is a vast expanse of wisdom (for lack of a more concise description) resting beyond my right shoulder, dripping into my consciousness and filling my entire self with its clarity. It is such a beautiful space to experience. It is larger than the library of congress, of all the books of all the lands, and yet it is as simple as a 3x5 card.

SING.

Take a nice deep breath. Stretch your shoulders, neck, uncross your legs and find that sore spot to focus on – release your breath with intention. It takes but a moment. Breathe in deep, don't restrict, just fill your abdomen. A full breath is a gift of life to your body, it nourishes your cells, it fills you with energy. If your breath is always shallow, you will never be full, never be satisfied and always be left wanting.

Take a nice deep breath.

KNOW.

I have nearly destroyed this pen, pushing the nib into the top. Holding the pen straight to write these pages. My hand has adapted to the changes of this pen, refusing to choose another pen, though I count at least ten scattered across my desk. I have become attached and loyal to the damage I have done to this pen. It is known, and so I adapt and bend to what it needs over myself. The new pen is unknown.

SPARKLE.

What do I need to take with me. What is a true necessity. What do I pack for safety, security, for just in case. What if I carry a lighter load. What if I don't lug all this weight with me, managing all this stuff. Surely there are non-negotiables – those things that keep me alive. The rest is added nonsense. I need very little, and every extra thing is a worry, a what if... Perhaps I should leave the worries home this trip.

GO.

Seeing the vision and finding the path are different phases in our journey. If you imagine the possible futures you have, there is a spotlight on your end goal. If you imagine your next step, you can only see just in front of you as you proceed on your journey. There is a winding way through the forest, and you can't see the detours and fallen logs around the next bend. How does one keep the vision in view when mired in the small steps forward each day.

REST.

We all follow the same path to the exit. We are born. We die. The body's role is fairly straight forward. In the middle we search. We seek understanding. We hide because it is scary. We resist because we aren't paying attention. We fight hard and protest when we discover what we missed so long ago. Then we see. We learn. We find what we need, and it is time to go. To go, take what we learned and help others. Help ourselves.

124

LISTEN.

Do you wonder, sitting quietly in the dark, what it is all about. Do you wonder when the day is long and tasks are many, why? Spoiler: it is not the tasks, it is not the things, it is not the achievement. All you are looking for is within. Behind the shelves of expectation and drawers stuffed with must dos. It is all there waiting for you in the silence.

CLIMB.

And so, in the darkness of the sleeping day, my thoughts run deep and clear. The muse is open, the ideas run free. The only thing lacking is more time. Time is truly the finite resource. How we use the time is a big, long conundrum. Our daily tasks eat a chunk that we will not remember – they are in service of keeping us organized and free from the clutter of our thoughts and spaces. How do we use the balance? Certainly, in service to others. A large part of my time is gifted to others besides me. I must learn to keep what I can.

LOOK.

I continue to be enraptured by the caramel color in my cup this morning. This perfect silky hue. I have never felt quite so distracted staring at a color. Is it that it indicates a perfect balance of coffee and cream? It is such a luxurious color, soft yet solid. Rich yet forgiving. The coffee is dark and lacks any bitterness. I want to wrap myself in its warmth and perfection. I want to dive into this color.

SELF.

I do not like tension in my shoulders keeping me stiff and unable to fully move. Tension filled with decisions, discussions and anticipation of something negative. This tension is so difficult to remove, its sticky mastic oozing through all the crevices of my cells leaving no room to let me be free. And when the decision is made, and the discussion is done, the stickiness releases its poison into my body in relief and exhaustion. I would much rather keep it away.

SOFT.

When your kindness extends beyond your bubble, beyond your overlapping circles of interest and influence, there are riches to be found. Life is a million moments, but each happens only once, and this is the only moment that is now. Why would you fill this moment with anything other than love. Be kind to those whose moments you share. Make eye contact. Say hello.

CARE.

The work is exhausting, looking within. It is dark and often full of scary things. If you focus outward, they don't make noises. They are muffled beneath all the shiny distractions. They are heavy, these items stored in boxes and unlabeled crates of your memory. They are hard to open when you spend years locking them away. And they are rotting. Their black mold is eating away your energy. It is draining looking within but each time, bring your light, clear the gunk layer by layer.

HYDRATE.

Each of us has our own circle of influence that overlaps and intersects with others. A day here, a moment there that our lives impact each other. A week together or a month or years of overlap. Each of us on our own path and our own direction, constantly – often subtly changing course based upon the words spoken or action completed by others. What a straight line we would travel if we never interacted with others. And aren't the wobbles what make it interesting.

QUESTION.

When you find a clue it may feel like a scrap, like a loose part that seems familiar, but you are not quite sure what it belongs to. A clue is but a glimpse and may not be needed for the puzzle of your life for years. Collect them all and noodle on them regularly. Left or right, up or down. You may find that piece fits exactly when you need it. Keep it safe.

CONNECT.

In this quiet peace of a Saturday morning, in the darkness of the world outside this window – there is nothing. All that exists in this moment is before me. These thoughts so incompletely captured. This pen bleeding its ink onto the page of this journal – this journal of expectations. What we value of things like this journal. It is lovely and given in love, so it becomes precious and the ego demands it be filled with philosophies large enough to meet the weight of that love.

I was wrong. In the darkness, beyond this space before me, outside this window – there is love.

DEEP.

The silence is so loud this morning that I turned on the music to drown out the noise. The music is a gatehouse, a security detail that filters the silence of the thoughts racing through. I long to sit quietly in the silence, and when I am out of practice there is not room for its vastness. Like training your muscles, you must train yourself to sit in the silence and allow its strength. When you fall into the silence, it will envelope your whole being.

OBSERVE.

Stick with what you know. Seek the knowledge for what you hope to understand. Do not put words into another's mouth. Do not steal a likeness that is not your own work, not your own face. Be decent. Be kind. Wonder what it would be like to walk another's path. Allow yourself to question the view from another's seat. Be curious. Adventure comes in many forms – the hardest one to start is the one that sees an opportunity to change your own mind. It is a scary cavern and one worth exploring.

LOOSEN.

You never can tell when an opportunity will present itself to show you that you have found the right path for this portion of your journey. That your voice could be muffled but need to be heard. How amazing it is to be put in a place where you encounter such an obstacle and realize that <u>you</u> have every skill you need to advance, and every confidence to guide another and help them along their journey. That you are the hero.

WRITE.

What makes us feel warm? Not the physical sensation of a fire on a cold night or a cup of tea and a blanket, but the soul enveloping warmth of kindness and safety. The security and comfort of warmth where you can let your muscles relax and you don't feel on guard all the time. When there is no threat and you can easily let your mind wander in conversation or in contemplation, with friendship and regard for the people you are with. This warmth is a healing magic salve.

LISTEN.

I want to know all the wisdom within, I want to be the holder of the information and have the answer. I want to dive into this pool of history and experience and let the thoughts seep through my pores, spilling out from my pen, sounding smart when I speak them. My eyes well up when I scratch the surface of all this information. When I am on the path meant for me, I feel it in my bones, through my body and it's like it's been there all along. It has.

GATHER.

I thought I should sit and write for two cups of coffee. Today I forgot to drink and so my first cup went cold. Not once did I think, I have been here too long. It is a two cup of coffee kind of day, so I wrapped my cold hand around the cold mug and wondered how long it has been. Has my playlist repeated? It is still dark outside. Where have all these words come from? I simply put them on the page. One cup of coffee at a time.

DO.

On a scrap of paper, with any pen – draw a shape. A square, an oval. Draw it quickly without thinking too hard.

Take a deep breath and exhale. Draw a line through your shape from one side to the other.

Take a deep breath. As you exhale, slowly draw another parallel line. Pick up your pen and start again. Take a breath, slowly exhale and draw a line. Repeat, filling your shape in a slow, purposeful line meditation.

HOLD.

Listen loudly to the voices in the dark. They tell you how to resolve the thing that scares you the most. Listen loudly when two ideas come together in a new way, they show you how to solve the problem, or at least start down a different path of resolution. Listen loudly to the words you don't want to hear – they tell you what you need to know. Listen loudly to the wisdom you hold, drowned out by the noise of life.

158

SIT.

Each day we wake to tackle our agenda, to go forward – faster, richer, better. Each day we wake and start on auto pilot. When we don't pause and listen to our inner voices – we do a disservice to ourselves. We must stop and listen. We must allow the deep recesses of wisdom within to bubble to the top of our consciousness. The wisdom is beneath layers of worries, stress, to dos. And the wisdom can guide us to find the better path of balance and harmony we crave.

WELCOME.

Today –is not the day I awoke to. I spent much of my time already in a different day, thinking and planning based on a mistaken awareness of the calendar. It matters not that today is not the day I think it is. For I am here, I am doing my things and living my life. Today will pass, the sun will rise, the moon will too eventually. It matters not whether it is Tuesday, or it is Friday. The time will pass.

STRETCH.

Take a deep breath in. Close your eyes for a moment, then release. Take another deep breath and shrug your shoulders up, back, down. Flex your neck and back to the left and to the right. Check your feet. Are they crossed and bound up? Are your legs wrapped around each other or feet flat on the floor. Are you comfortable? Hold your mug in your hands and feel its warmth. A personal hand warmer. Or perhaps your favorite pen is near. Or this book. Take a moment to marvel at your morning.

PAUSE.

PONDER.

CARE.

A sore muscle from a hard day's work is a fairly satisfactory feeling. It tells a story of movement and exertion, perhaps sweat, of accomplishment. A sore muscle from a hard day's work makes you feel part of this place, doing the work it takes to survive, to thrive. Doing this myself. A sore muscle from gardening, lifting, organizing, building, fixing, pushing, or pulling screams – I am part of this world.

CREATE.

In this space the world has an opportunity to make sense. There are no other opinions. There are no other distractions. Things to do wait for me on the other side of the door. The world's problems still go on, and here my deep breaths, my ability to breathe fully and true calm my nerves for what I can control. There is no input in this magical space, deep in the dark morning. It is just me. I am the center of the universe in this space.

QUIET.

I need to have more shots in the dark in my day. It affects no one to do so. It employs minimal effort. It makes me happy. A small treat, a hug, a lovely-just for me and myself. It is kindness in a cup of warmth and creates such happiness with each sip. With each grip of the mug, when the elixir reaches my lips, it is like a kiss of flavor for me alone. It is a secret, this extra boost of flavor and I am worth a little something more. I am deserving of this luxury for myself.

OPEN.

I searched for home for many years, feeling unsettled, not having a sense of place. I searched for home – lost in the idea that a roof was what I needed. Just not this roof or that. Through unrest, unhappiness, dissatisfaction, I tried new ways to make these walls home. That was the wrong journey. I found home, the sense of stability, safety and warmth when I sought to find myself.

DRAW.

Each time I close this book a chill runs through and I pick up the pen again to capture what there is to say. The room is cold in this early morning, but the chill is not from the room. It is an old friend, a physical manifestation of a message received, a notification ding from the energy that I am interpreting what is being shared. I have heard the thoughts before but only when I learned to listen did I get the chill.

APPRECIATE.

I should not feel as though I am frantic and rushed because of the clock. It is almost always outside forces that cause the craziness of feeling like you might miss out or be late. Appointments, meetings, expectations. I want to be in this soft space of early morning and let the day unfold, let my next activity dictate the way time develops. It is only rarely on a Sunday where that is allowed to happen, and only because I created that rule for myself. But the early morning quiet before the world wakes should be my relaxed state of always.

LISTEN.

In normal history the answers have been sought. We have taken journeys across lands in a pilgrimage to find the reasons. Our heroes have faced obstacles and setbacks. Our fables tell the journey story across cultures and continents. Never has such a powerful foe been our adversary as the foe we hold in our hands, that we devote a disproportionate number of hours to. Never have we willingly given up our freedoms of thought and time to become slaves to a device.

ASK.

Our battles are not a straight path, they are not prescribed and part of a recipe to follow. The battles begin with what we are witness to, what we carry with us and what we can leave behind. Some things will be easier to leave, some burdens will be harder. You become used to their weight, and they are part of your identity. You will climb hills with them and watch the sunrise holding them and one day you may set them down, and continue on your journey with new strength and capacity to carry what comes next.

WONDER.

Visits from a friend are not always life changing. They need not be epic in nature and activity. The time together may be routine and comforting. The days may just be time. Companionship. Love. Company. Being present with each other. Eye to eye. Hand in hand. A meal, a cup of tea or just time. What is left is a cushion of fondness. A protection against the next harm to come your way. A buffer against the harshness of the world. Visits from a friend are a lingering softness when things feel hard.

SMILE.

When you listen, there is a softening of your thoughts. At first, they will run round like children on the playground but eventually they will tire. Eventually you can tuck them away. This requires patience and grace. Your thoughts will run from here to there stirring up worries and fears, distracting you from listening, making it impossible to listen. But your patience and grace returns each time and then one day there will be a moment when your thoughts quiet enough for your first moment of listening.

BREATHE.

THIS IS NEVER

THE

END

CHRONOLOGICAL INDEX

www.ingramcontent.com/pod-product-compliance
Lightning Source LLC
Chambersburg PA
CBHW031501160726
47994CB00005B/2143